# Twenty to Make

# Button Jewellery

## Marrianne Mercer

Search Press

First published in Great Britain 2011

Search Press Limited
Wellwood, North Farm Road,
Tunbridge Wells, Kent TN2 3DR

Reprinted 2012

Text copyright © Marrianne Mercer 2011

Photographs by Debbie Patterson at
Search Press Studios

Photographs and design copyright
© Search Press Ltd 2011

ISBN 978 1 84448 654 0

### Suppliers

If you have difficulty in obtaining any of the
materials and equipment mentioned in this book,
then please visit the Search Press website for
details of suppliers: www.searchpress.com

Printed in Malaysia

*Dedication*
*To my Mum and Dad, who have always*
*encouraged my creativity.*

## A note on buttons

*There are many varieties of button available on
the market, and although I specify what kind
of button to use in each project, please use
you imagination and if you can't find the exact
colour or size, use something similar and adapt
the design accordingly. Buttons can be very
expensive, so shop around.*

*I found it much easier to source what I needed
online; do a search for buttons in a search
engine. ebay shops are also very
good and those dedicated to crafts or just
buttons are excellent at keeping specific buttons
in stock.*

*If the internet isn't your thing, then many
haberdashery stores stock a great array of
buttons, as do specialist art and craft shops.
Buttons can also be bought from papercraft
sections in shops, as they are used to adorn
handmade cards.*

# Contents

Introduction  4

Materials and tools  6

Diagrams  7

Cotton Thong Necklace  8

Old World Charm  10

Rings 'n' Things  12

Toggle Bracelet  14

Seaside Shell Earrings  16

Trio Necklace  18

Vintage Charm Bracelet  20

Chained Button Necklace  22

Golden Age Earrings  24

Stacked Boho Necklace  26

Layered Bracelet  28

Three-String Necklace  30

Mini Button Earrings  32

Dangly Rings  34

Long Cluster Necklace  36

Daisy Bangle  38

Criss-Cross Bracelet  40

Stacked Earrings  42

Glasses String  44

Stacked Necklace  46

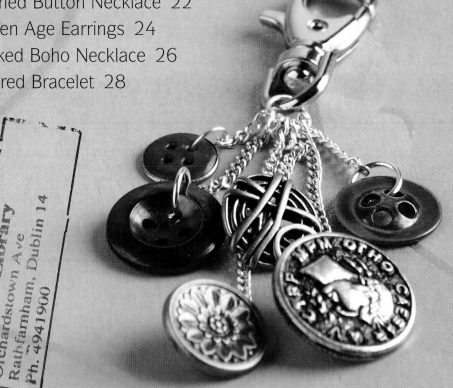

# Introduction

After taking a day course in beaded jewellery making, I was hooked, but I would never have believed that it would lead me to writing my own book.

Buttons are not something you notice until they become the subject of a project. There really are thousands out there of varying colours, shapes and sizes and combinations of them can be used to create a beautiful, fun and charming piece of jewellery.

I hope in this book I can teach you how to use simple and some more complex beading techniques, and how to integrate those with buttons.

I had lots of fun thinking up these original designs and really hope that while I use a particular size and colour of button, you also become imaginative with the buttons you use. You can change colour schemes or add some textured, metal or wooden buttons to create a completely different look, so let your imagination run wild.

It is also a great idea to raid your mother's, grandmother's or next door neighbour's button tin, not only because this is recycling, but also because it helps to save on cost and creates a unique piece of jewellery.

I hope you gain as much satisfaction from making jewellery as I do.
Good luck.

# Materials and tools

Below I have listed the staple materials and tools that will help to get you started in jewellery making.

**1 Ruler** This helps you to measure and cut lengths of wire and cord.

**2 Wire cutters** Use these to cut jewellery or craft wire.

**3 Flat-nosed pliers** These help to flatten crimp beads, hold wires in position and open and close jump rings.

**4 Round-nosed pliers** These help to create smooth loops of wire, and to finish off wire-wrapped loops.

**5 Snipe (chain)-nosed pliers** Used to hold jump rings and to close cord end crimps.

**6 Scissors** These are for cutting cord or elastic.

**7 Variety of chains** Chain can be purchased in all kinds of sizes, shapes and colours.

**8 Flexible beading wire** This is made up of a number of fine, flexible wires coated in plastic for durability.

**9 Leather thong** A softer, durable alternative to chain.

**10 Strong elastic beading cord** This is for stretchy bracelets and can be cotton-covered (as shown below) or transparent.

**11 Cotton-coated memory wire** A colourful, workable and attractive variation to jewellery or craft wire.

**12 Cotton thong** A good material to use for colourful or longer jewellery styles.

**13 Necklace cones** Use these to link together more than one string of beads or buttons.

**14 Swivel clip** These are excellent for charms.

**15 Head pins and eye pins** These help to link buttons and beads on to chain.

**16 Findings** These include earring hooks, cord end crimps, lobster clasps, stud earrings and butterflies, jump rings, split rings, bolt rings and crimp beads.

**17 Beading mat** This helps to stop materials rolling on to the floor.

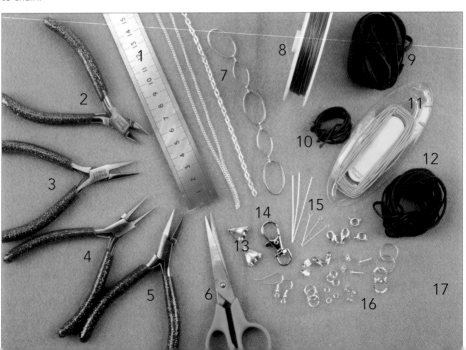

# Diagrams

**Diagram 1**
*A single overhand knot.*

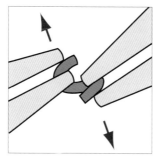

**Diagram 2**
*Opening a jump ring.*

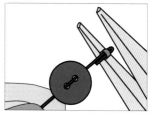

**Diagram 3**
*Flattening a crimp.*

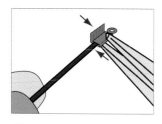

**Diagram 4**
*Flattening a cord end crimp.*

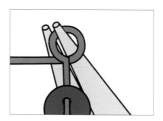

**Diagram 5**
*1. To make a wire-wrapped loop, first wrap the wire in a loop around one jaw of a pair of round-nosed pliers.*

*2. Wrap the wire back round the main leg two or three times to secure.*

**Diagram 6**
*A lark's head knot.*

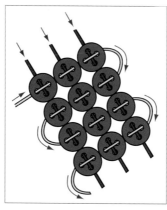

**Diagram 7**
*A criss-cross bracelet.*

# Cotton Thong Necklace

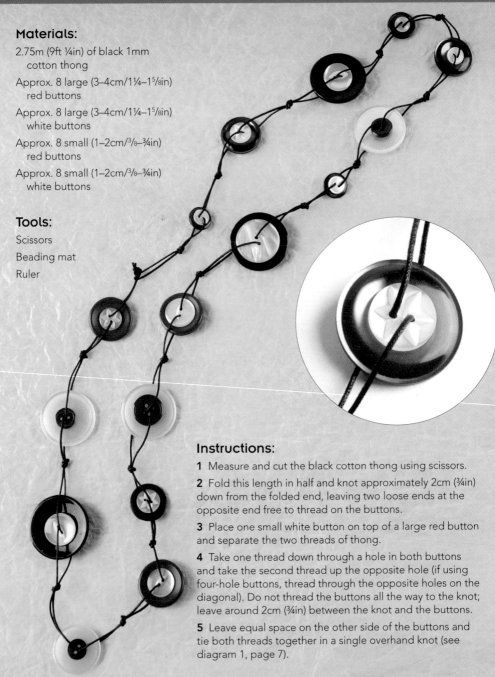

## Materials:

2.75m (9ft ¼in) of black 1mm
  cotton thong

Approx. 8 large (3–4cm/1¼–1⅝in)
  red buttons

Approx. 8 large (3–4cm/1¼–1⅝in)
  white buttons

Approx. 8 small (1–2cm/⅜–¾in)
  red buttons

Approx. 8 small (1–2cm/⅜–¾in)
  white buttons

## Tools:

Scissors

Beading mat

Ruler

## Instructions:

**1** Measure and cut the black cotton thong using scissors.

**2** Fold this length in half and knot approximately 2cm (¾in) down from the folded end, leaving two loose ends at the opposite end free to thread on the buttons.

**3** Place one small white button on top of a large red button and separate the two threads of thong.

**4** Take one thread down through a hole in both buttons and take the second thread up the opposite hole (if using four-hole buttons, thread through the opposite holes on the diagonal). Do not thread the buttons all the way to the knot; leave around 2cm (¾in) between the knot and the buttons.

**5** Leave equal space on the other side of the buttons and tie both threads together in a single overhand knot (see diagram 1, page 7).

**6** Follow steps 3 to 5 using different combinations of button colour and size (as shown) until you reach the ends of the threads.

**7** Once at the end, take one thread through the starting loop and join it with the other thread by tying it with a double overhand knot (see diagram 1, page 7 and repeat). Your necklace should now be secure. Wear it as a long single strand or double it for texture.

### Out of the Woods
*Wooden beads and brown cotton thong make a beautiful, natural-looking necklace. For those who don't like too much dangle, make it shorter.*

# Old World Charm

## Materials:

31cm (12¼in) gold-plated
  curb chain

6 vintage shank buttons of
  varying sizes (1–2cm/³⁄₈–¾in)

1 x 7mm (⁵⁄₁₆in) gold-plated
  jump ring

7 x 5mm (³⁄₁₆in) gold-plated
  jump rings

1 gold-plated swivel clip

## Tools:

Wire cutters

Flat-nosed pliers

Snipe (chain)-nosed pliers

Beading mat

Ruler

## Instructions:

**1** Use wire cutters to cut the chain into six lengths, 2 x 6cm (2³⁄₈in), 1 x 7cm (2¾in), 2 x 4.5cm (1¾in) and 1 x 3cm (1¼in).

**2** Thread the last link of each length of chain on to one 5mm (³⁄₁₆in) jump ring. Open and close the jump ring using the flat-nosed and snipe-nosed pliers (see diagram 2, page 7).

**3** Now join the chains to the swivel clip using the 7mm (⁵⁄₁₆in) jump ring. You should now have a charm without the buttons attached.

**4** To add the buttons to the chains, use a 5mm (³⁄₁₆in) jump ring looped through the shank of each button and also through the last link on each chain. Use the larger buttons on the longer chains so they do not cover the smaller buttons.

# Silver Service

*Continue the vintage appeal in an old silver colour scheme. Here I have used some vintage silver and new pewter buttons to change the look.*

# Rings 'n' Things

## Materials:

18mm (¾in) yellow button

14mm (⁹⁄₁₆in) green button

11mm (⁷⁄₁₆in) pink button

2.5cm (1in) DMC turquoise
memory wire

Flat-based adjustable
silver-plated ring finding

## Tools:

Wire cutters or scissors

Strong liquid jewellery glue

Beading mat

Ruler

## Instructions:

**1** Lay the buttons in a stack, yellow at the bottom, then green and pink on top.

**2** Cut a 2.5cm (1in) length of DMC wire using wire cutters or scissors.

**3** Thread the wire up through the buttons and back down the other hole, so the wire ends are both on the underside of the yellow button.

**4** Bend the wire ends over towards one another against the button base to hold the buttons in place.

**5** Spread plenty of glue on the flat top of the ring finding and on the wire ends on the bottom of the yellow button. Place together as centrally as possible. Be careful not to get glue on any visible areas as it can leave a white residue when dry. If this happens the excess glue can sometimes be removed with plenty of nail varnish remover.

# Cuff Links and Stud Earrings

*Many items of jewellery can be made using similar techniques. Thread some beads on to head pins and fold underneath the buttons for a funky Martian-looking ring variation, or use just the jewellery glue to attach buttons to cuff link findings or stud earrings. Cut off any unwanted button shanks with nail clippers or side wire cutters.*

# Toggle Bracelet

## Materials:

46cm (18in) of 0.7mm strong elastic beading cord

Approx 19 x 2.5cm (1in) beech tube toggle buttons

Approx 19 x 2.5cm (1in) beech flat toggle buttons

2 x 2mm ($^1/_{16}$in) silver-plated crimp beads

## Tools:

Flat-nosed pliers

Scissors

Beading mat

Ruler

## Instructions:

**1** Cut two 23cm (9in) lengths of strong elastic beading cord using scissors.

**2** Thread on the toggle buttons, alternating the tubes and flat ones, through one of the two holes. Thread the other length of cord through the other set of holes so that the buttons all sit evenly in a line.

**3** Once all the buttons are threaded on, put a crimp bead on one of the ends of cord, then thread the other end of the same piece through the crimp bead from the opposite direction. Try not to stretch the cord. Flatten the crimp bead using the flat-nosed pliers (see diagram 3, page 7) as close to the toggles as you can.

**4** Test whether the crimp is holding the cord securely by stretching the bracelet gently, and repeat the same crimping process on the second piece of cord.

**5** Cut off any excess cord ends using scissors.

# Reggae Twist

*Make a chunky bracelet using 40mm (1⅝in) toggle buttons. These multicoloured toggle buttons teamed with dark walnut toggles give a hot Caribbean feel.*

# Seaside Shell Earrings

## Materials:

8 x 10mm (³⁄₈in) silver-
  plated jump rings

4 x 5mm (³⁄₁₆in) silver-
  plated jump rings

2 x 4cm (1⁵⁄₈in) silver-
  plated chain

2 x silver-plated earring
  hooks

4 x 18mm (¾in) shell
  buttons

2 x 15mm (⁵⁄₈in)
  turquoise buttons

## Tools:

Flat-nosed pliers

Wire cutters

Snipe (chain)-nosed pliers

Scissors

Beading mat

Ruler

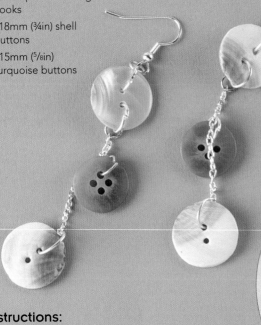

## Instructions:

**1** Attach a 10mm (³⁄₈in) jump ring through one of the
holes in a shell button (see diagram 2, page 7). Attach to
this a 5mm (³⁄₁₆in) jump ring, and then an earring finding on
to that.

**2** Add another 10mm (³⁄₈in) jump ring through the other hole in
the same button and attach to that a 5mm (³⁄₁₆in) jump ring and a
4cm (1⁵⁄₈in) length of chain.

**3** On the other end of the chain attach another shell button with a 10mm
(³⁄₈in) jump ring.

**4** Now use another 10mm (³⁄₈in) jump ring to attach a turquoise button
around one-third of the way down the chain so that it hangs centrally between
the two shell buttons.

**5** Repeat all the above steps for the second earring.

## Bronzed Beauty

*Warm to the seaside theme by using bronze-coloured shell buttons with wooden buttons and gold chain.*

# Trio Necklace

## Materials:

36cm (14¼in) brown leather thong

3 x 4cm (1⅝in) chunky wooden buttons

3 x 20mm (¾in) green two-hole buttons

2 x 2mm (¹⁄₁₆in) crimp beads

6 x silver-plated cord end crimps

1 x 9mm (⅜in) silver-plated
lobster clasp

1 x 6mm (¼in) silver-plated split ring

4 x 5mm (³⁄₁₆in) silver-plated
jump rings

22cm (8⅝in) DMC white
memory wire

## Tools:

Flat-nosed pliers

Wire cutters

Snipe (chain)-
nosed pliers

Scissors

Beading mat

Ruler

## Instructions:

**1** Cut the leather thong in half using scissors.

**2** On each end of both lengths of thong attach a cord end crimp. It is a bit fiddly but use the snipe-nosed pliers to push the sides of the cord end crimp over on top of the thong (see diagram 4, page 7).

**3** Add a jump ring (see diagram 2, page 7) and a split ring to one end of the first length of thong.

**4** Attach a jump ring and lobster clasp to one end of the second length of thong. Now open the lobster clasp and attach it to the split ring on the other piece of thong.

**5** Stack the green buttons on top of the large wooden buttons and place in a row.

**6** Thread the buttons together using the length of memory wire, starting from the back, making sure each stack only just touches the next. Try to leave 2.5cm (1in) of memory wire at either end of the row.

**7** Add a crimp bead on to either end of the memory wire and place it as close to the button hole as you can before flattening it with your flat-nosed pliers (see diagram 3, page 7). This helps keep the buttons in place on the memory wire.

**8** Add a cord end crimp to either end of the wire, close to the edge of the buttons. Cut off any excess wire.

**9** Join the trio of buttons to the leather thong using a jump ring to link both sets of cord ends.

**Loving Summer**
*Bring on the feeling of summer using brightly coloured buttons with gingham ribbon.*

# Vintage Charm Bracelet

## Materials:

Selection of approximately 22 vintage shank buttons in varying sizes

18cm (7⅛in) gold-plated chain

22 x 6mm (¼in) gold-plated jump rings

24 x 4mm (⅛in) gold-plated jump rings

1 gold-plated bolt ring and fastener

## Tools:

Flat-nosed pliers

Round-nosed pliers

Wire cutters

Beading mat

Ruler

## Finished length:

19.5cm (7¾in) including clasp. Vary the length of chain and the number of buttons to suit the wearer.

## Instructions:

**1** Attach the bolt ring clasp and fastener to either ends of the chain using 4mm (⅛in) jump rings (see diagram 2, page 7).

**2** Attach a 6mm (¼in) jump ring to each button shank, and then attach that to a 4mm (⅛in) jump ring. The smaller jump rings are used because they will be threaded through the chain links later – the larger jump rings will be too thick.

**3** Attach a button to every fourth or sixth link in the chain (depending on how large the button is), by threading small jump rings, already attached, through a link in the chain. Obviously the larger the button is, the more space it needs either side.

# Flower Power

*Use flower shank buttons with other brightly coloured buttons and silver chain for a young, fresh and summery look.*

# Chained Button Necklace

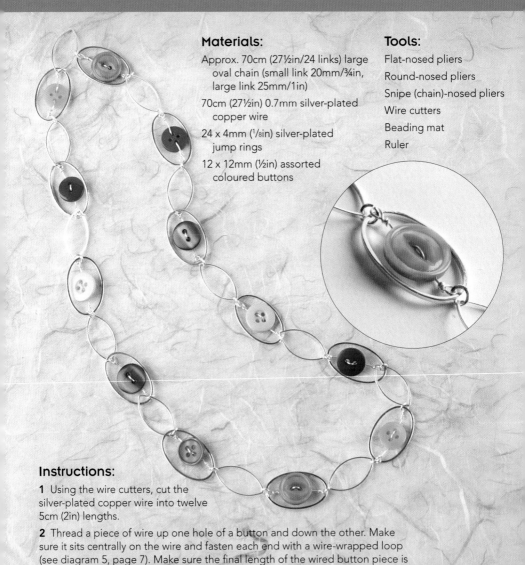

## Materials:

Approx. 70cm (27½in/24 links) large
    oval chain (small link 20mm/¾in,
    large link 25mm/1in)

70cm (27½in) 0.7mm silver-plated
    copper wire

24 x 4mm (⅛in) silver-plated
    jump rings

12 x 12mm (½in) assorted
    coloured buttons

## Tools:

Flat-nosed pliers

Round-nosed pliers

Snipe (chain)-nosed pliers

Wire cutters

Beading mat

Ruler

## Instructions:

**1** Using the wire cutters, cut the
silver-plated copper wire into twelve
5cm (2in) lengths.

**2** Thread a piece of wire up one hole of a button and down the other. Make
sure it sits centrally on the wire and fasten each end with a wire-wrapped loop
(see diagram 5, page 7). Make sure the final length of the wired button piece is
approximately 2.5cm (1in), to fit inside the large oval chain links.

**3** Continue wiring all of the buttons in the same way.

**4** Unlink the large oval chain. Open a jump ring (see diagram 2, page 7) and
thread on one large oval chain link and one wired button. Close the jump ring.

**5** Open another jump ring and thread the other end of the wired button through
it along with the other side of the oval. This time also add a small oval link and
close the jump ring.

**6** Next open another jump ring and thread it on to the opposite end of the small oval link, along with another large oval link and a wired button, and close the jump ring.

**7** Continue this sequence until all of the large and small oval links are placed back together. No clasp is needed as it should slip over your head.

### Ocean Breeze

*Keep the colour scheme simple with aqua and blue buttons. Here the unusual square buttons bring a fresh, modern approach to the design.*

# Golden Age Earrings

## Materials:

2 x gold-plated earring hooks

2 x 5cm (2in) gold-plated eye pins

2 x 14mm (⁹/₁₆in) vintage
   gold buttons

4 x gold-plated rose detail beads

## Tools:

Flat-nosed pliers

Round-nosed pliers

Wire cutters

Beading mat

## Instructions:

**1** Thread one rose bead on to an eye pin, followed by one of the vintage buttons, followed again by a rose bead.

**2** Fasten the eye pin with a wire-wrapped loop (see diagram 5, page 7).

**3** Now attach the earring hook to the wire-wrapped loop, opening the loop of the earring hook as you would a jump ring (see diagram 2, page 7).

**4** Repeat for the second earring.

# Silver Stars

*Use star-shaped beads and buttons in vintage silver and deep blue to add a little bit of wizardry.*

# Stacked Boho Necklace

## Materials:

20cm (7⅞in) of 0.7mm flexible
  beading wire

36cm (14⅛in) silver-plated
  textured chain

4 x 4mm (⅛in) silver-plated jump rings

1 x 11mm (⁷⁄₁₆in) silver-plated
  lobster clasp

1 x 6mm (¼in) silver-plated split ring

2 x 2mm (¹⁄₁₆in) silver-plated
  crimp beads

Selection of approximately 35 green
  buttons in varying sizes and shades

## Tools:

Flat-nosed pliers

Snipe (chain-)nosed pliers

Wire cutters

Beading mat

Ruler

## Instructions:

**1** Fold the flexible beading wire in half. Thread one crimp bead and one jump ring on to the open ends and fold the flexible beading wire ends back through the crimp bead to create a loop in which the jump ring sits. Try to do this as near to the end as possible. Flatten the crimp to secure it (see diagram 3, page 7).

**2** Cut the other, folded end of the flexible beading wire to create two strands.

**3** Thread all of the buttons in no particular order on to the strands of flexible beading wire, making sure both strands go through the same hole.

**4** Fasten the end of the flexible beading wire in the same way as in step 1, using a crimp bead and jump ring. Put to one side.

**5** Use wire cutters to cut the length of textured chain in half. Attach each half to one end of the button stack using the already attached jump rings (see diagram 2, page 7).

**6** Add a jump ring and split ring to one of the lengths and a jump ring and lobster clasp to the other length to finish.

### Boho Babe
*Add a little boho chic to your design with some colourful buttons teamed with a brass look chain.*

# Layered Bracelet

## Materials:

30cm (11⅞in) of white DMC memory wire

2 x silver-plated cord end crimps

1 x 9mm (³⁄₈in) silver-plated lobster clasp

1 x 6mm (¼in) silver-plated split ring

2 x 4mm (⅛in) silver-plated jump rings

3 x 28mm (1⅛in) white buttons

3 x 28mm (1⅛in) black buttons

3 x 22mm (⅞in) black and white check buttons

3 x 8mm (⁵⁄₁₆in) red heart buttons

## Tools:

Flat-nosed pliers

Snipe (chain)-nosed pliers

Wire cutters or scissors

Beading mat

Ruler

## Finished length:

19cm (7½in) including clasp. Vary the length of thread and the number of buttons to suit the wearer.

## Instructions:

**1** Attach a cord end crimp to one end of the length of memory wire (see diagram 4, page 7).

**2** Thread on one black and one red heart button, stacked, so they are close to the cord end, ensuring the thread is taught. Thread the remaining buttons on, alternating the white and chequered buttons, stacked together, with the black and red heart buttons.

**3** Attach the other cord end crimp to the other end of the memory wire and cut off any excess thread with scissors or wire cutters.

**4** Attach a jump ring (see diagram 2, page 7) and lobster clasp to one cord end and a jump ring and split ring to the opposite end to finish.

### It's all Peachy
*For a more subtle, feminine look, use pastel buttons with brightly coloured thread. This can look fun or elegant teamed with the right outfit.*

# Three-String Necklace

## Materials:

105cm (41½in) of 0.3 gauge flexible beading wire

2 x 2mm (¹⁄₁₆in) silver-plated crimp beads

2 x three-hole silver-plated necklace cones

3 x 5mm (³⁄₁₆in) silver-plated split rings

20cm (7⅞in) silver-plated chain

1 x 12mm (½in) silver-plated lobster clasp

2 x 4mm (⅛in) silver-plated jump rings

60 x 9mm (⅜in) pink buttons

60 x 9mm (⅜in) yellow buttons

60 x 9mm (⅜in) orange buttons

## Tools:

Flat-nosed pliers

Snipe (chain)-nosed pliers

Wire cutters

Beading mat

Ruler

## Instructions:

**1** Cut 1 x 30cm (11¾in), 1 x 35cm (13¾in) and 1 x 40cm (15¾in) lengths of flexible beading wire.

**2** Thread the lengths from short to long through the holes of one necklace cone.

**3** Thread a crimp bead and split ring through the three strings of flexible beading wire on the small end of the cone, then thread them back down the crimp bead and fasten them by flattening the crimp bead with flat-nosed pliers (see diagram 3, page 7). The split ring should now be fastened to the strings in a loop at the end.

**4** Thread one button of each colour on to the short necklace string until you have 51 buttons on it.

**5** Repeat on the second string with 60 buttons and on the third string with 69 buttons.

**6** Now thread each string back up the second necklace cone. Ensure the short string is on top and go down the cone in size order. Fasten as in step 3.

**7** Cut two 10cm (4in) pieces of chain. Attach one length to each split ring (at the end of the necklace cones) using a jump ring (see diagram 2, page 7).

**8** On one side of the chain attach a jump ring and lobster clasp and on the other side attach a jump ring and split ring to finish.

**Peacock Perfect**
Change the colour of the buttons to go with your favourite outfit. These chunky necklaces look great in the summer and add a splash of colour to your suntan.

# Mini Button Earrings

## Materials:

14cm (5½in) silver-plated medium size chain

2 x silver-plated earring hooks

38 x 6mm (¼in) silver-plated jump rings

38 x 6mm (¼in) buttons in varying colours

## Tools:

Flat-nosed pliers

Snipe (chain)-nosed pliers

Wire cutters

Beading mat

Ruler

## Instructions:

**1** Cut the chain in half using wire cutters.

**2** Attach an earring hook to one piece in the same way you would open and close a jump ring (see diagram 2, page 7).

**3** Now open a jump ring fairly wide and thread on a button, and then thread the jump ring through the last link in the chain. Close the jump ring.

**4** Leave one link empty and then repeat step 3 on the next link. Continue up the length of the chain until you have nineteen buttons attached.

**5** Repeat steps 2 to 4 for the second earring.

## Little Sweethearts

*Tiny heart buttons make these earrings an ideal gift for Valentine's Day, or just to dress up for a romantic occasion.*

# Dangly Rings

## Materials:

5 x 9mm (³/₈in) black buttons

5 x 4mm (¹/₈in) gold-plated
   diamante beads

1 x ten-loop gold-plated
   ring finding

10 x 6mm (¼in) jump rings

## Tools:

Flat-nosed pliers

Snipe (chain)-nosed pliers

Beading mat

## Instructions:

**1** Open a jump ring fairly wide (see diagram 2, page 7) and attach a black button, then thread it through the first loop on the ring. Close the jump ring.

**2** Open a jump ring and attach a diamante bead, then thread it through the second loop on the ring. Close the jump ring.

**3** Repeat steps 1 and 2 until all the loops have alternating buttons and beads attached to them.

### In the Pink

*For a more subtle daytime look, mix up some buttons in different tones of pink. Experiment with texture by using some shaped buttons too.*

# Long Cluster Necklace

## Materials:

10mm (³⁄₈in) silver-plated textured spacer ring

1 x 4mm (¹⁄₈in) silver-plated jump ring

5 x 6mm (¼in) silver-plated jump rings

3 x 10mm (³⁄₈in) silver-plated jump rings

2 x 15mm (⅝in) green buttons

2 x 15mm (⅝in) pink buttons

1 x 33mm (1⁵⁄₁₆in) green button

1 x 33mm (1⁵⁄₁₆in) pink button

1 x 33mm (1⁵⁄₁₆in) metal daisy shank button

43cm (17in) silver-plated textured oval chain

1m (39½in) bright pink leather thong

1m (39½in) lime green leather thong

## Tools:

Flat-nosed pliers

Snipe (chain)-nosed pliers

Wire cutters

Beading mat

Ruler

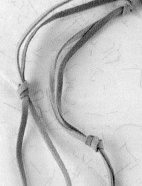

## Instructions:

**1** Use wire cutters to cut lengths of chain: 1 x 3cm (1¼in), 1 x 4cm (1⁵⁄₈in), 2 x 6cm (2³⁄₈in), 1 x 7cm (2¾in), 1 x 8cm (3¹⁄₈in) and 1 x 9cm (3½in).

**2** Link each button to the last link on a chain length with a jump ring (see diagram 2, page 7). Use the 10mm (³⁄₈in) jump rings with the 33mm (1⁵⁄₁₆in) buttons, and the 6mm (¼in) jump rings with the 15mm (⅝in) buttons and the daisy shank button. Note that the bigger buttons are more effective on the longer chain lengths.

**3** Arrange the chained buttons on the bead mat so the lengths and colours mix up and look uneven.

**4** When they are in a combination that pleases you, attach them one by one to a 10mm (³⁄₈in) jump ring. Close it and attach a 4mm (¹⁄₈in) jump ring.

**5** Now attach the textured spacer ring to the 4mm (¹⁄₈in) jump ring.

**6** Place both lengths of leather thong together and fold in half.

**7** Thread the folds through the textured spacer ring and loop the four cut ends of cord back through the loop on the other side so it knots around the spacer ring in a lark's head knot (see diagram 6, page 7).

**8** Tie an overhand single knot (see diagram 1, page 7) every 10cm (4in) up on either side of the necklace to hold the loose thongs together.

**9** Tie a tight double overhand knot to close the two ends of the thongs.

### Black and White Wonder
*For a really striking look, use just black and white and mix it with lots of geometric shapes and patterns. People won't believe you can get buttons like these!*

# Daisy Bangle

## Materials:

- 35cm (13¾in) of 1.5mm silver-plated copper wire
- 2.73m (8 ft 11½in) of 0.5mm silver-plated copper wire
- 4 x 5mm (³/₁₆in) silver-plated spacer beads
- 3 x metal daisy shank buttons

## Tools:

- Flat-nosed pliers
- Round-nosed pliers
- Wire cutters
- Liquid jewellery glue
- File
- Beading mat
- Ruler

## Instructions:

**1** Cut the 1.5mm wire to length and file the ends. This will become the core of the bracelet.

**2** Cut a 61cm (24in) length of the 0.5mm wire. Hold both wires 2cm (¾in) from the ends. Wrap the thinner wire around the core, keeping it very tight and not overlapping it.

**3** Once all the thin wire is wrapped around the core, cut any stray ends flush with the core and file any sharp ends. Bend in the thin wire ends so they sit close to the core using the flat-nosed pliers.

**4** Repeat steps 2 and 3 twice more.

**5** You should now have approximately 15cm (5⁷/₈in) of wire wrapped centrally on the core. Now thread three daisy shank buttons on to the centre of the wire-wrapped core.

**6** Secure the buttons by cutting a 10cm (4in) length of 0.5mm wire and wrapping it around the core in a criss-cross fashion surrounding the shank. Make sure the buttons are facing the same way.

**7** Place two spacer beads on one end of the remaining core and then wrap the next 2cm (¾in) of core, with 30cm (11¾in) of the thinner wire. Do not wrap right to the end of the core. Do this on both ends.

**8** Use round-nosed pliers to curl the ends of the bangle in tightly to create opposite facing spirals. Try to make sure the wrapped wire stays close to the beads and doesn't move to the end of the core wire.

**9** Now bend the bangle into the shape of your wrist as smoothly as you can.

**10** Dab a small amount of jewellery glue on to the underside of your buttons to secure firmly in place. Leave to dry.

**Celtic Treasure**
*If you prefer something steeped in ancient history, then try using bronze wire with a metal Celtic style button.*

# Criss-Cross Bracelet

## Materials:

2m (79in) red DMC memory wire

6 x silver-plated cord end crimps

1 x 24mm (¹⁵/₁₆in) silver-plated three-strand clasp

6 x 4mm (¹/₈in) silver-plated jump rings

60 x 9mm (³/₈in) black four-hole buttons

## Tools:

Flat-nosed pliers

Snipe (chain)-nosed pliers

Wire cutters or scissors

Beading mat

Ruler

## Instructions:

**1** Cut 3 x 35cm (13¾in) lengths of red DMC memory wire.

**2** Thread twenty buttons on to each length of wire as closely as possible, leaving space at each end of the row to fasten into a cord end.

**3** Place the rows of buttons side by side on the beading mat. With the remaining memory wire, thread through the empty holes to make a cross of wire on the top of each button. Thread the wire across the three buttons of the first row, then down on to the next row and continue along the three strands of buttons in a zigzag pattern so that they pull together tightly into a wide band of buttons (see diagram 7, page 7).

**4** When you get to the end, fasten the wires from each row of buttons into a cord end crimp (see diagram 4, page 7). Some cord end crimps will need to hold two wires where the fourth zigzagging wire started and ended. Cut off any excess wire.

**5** Now attach the cord end crimps to the clasp using jump rings (see diagram 2, page 7).

**Bright and Beautiful**
*Add colour and shine to this design
by using a selection of brightly-
coloured buttons with a pearly
shine and contrasting black wire.*

# Stacked Earrings

## Materials:

4 x 3mm (⅛in) gold-plated spacer beads

2 x 55mm (2⅛in) gold-plated head pins

16 x 9mm (⅜in) wooden clown buttons

2 x gold-plated earring hooks

## Tools:

Round-nosed pliers

Wire cutters

Beading mat

## Instructions:

**1** Thread one spacer bead and eight buttons on to a head pin, followed by another spacer bead.

**2** With round-nosed pliers, fasten the end of the head pin with a wire-wrapped loop (see diagram 5, page 7).

**3** Open the earring hook as you would a jump ring (see diagram 2, page 7) and thread it on. Close the loop to finish.

**4** Repeat steps 1 to 3 for the second earring.

## Cool Blue Ocean
*Try using silver-plated head pins and earring hooks with square buttons in cool sea blues to give a really fresh look.*

# Glasses String

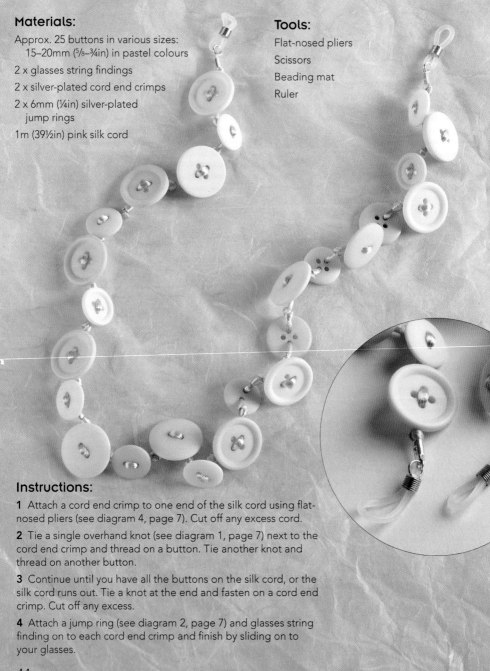

## Materials:

Approx. 25 buttons in various sizes:
   15–20mm (⅝–¾in) in pastel colours

2 x glasses string findings

2 x silver-plated cord end crimps

2 x 6mm (¼in) silver-plated
   jump rings

1m (39½in) pink silk cord

## Tools:

Flat-nosed pliers

Scissors

Beading mat

Ruler

## Instructions:

**1** Attach a cord end crimp to one end of the silk cord using flat-nosed pliers (see diagram 4, page 7). Cut off any excess cord.

**2** Tie a single overhand knot (see diagram 1, page 7) next to the cord end crimp and thread on a button. Tie another knot and thread on another button.

**3** Continue until you have all the buttons on the silk cord, or the silk cord runs out. Tie a knot at the end and fasten on a cord end crimp. Cut off any excess.

**4** Attach a jump ring (see diagram 2, page 7) and glasses string finding on to each cord end crimp and finish by sliding on to your glasses.

## Sparkling Spectacles

*Give yourself a sophisticated glasses string for an evening out using black cord and buttons with gold diamante beads. Use a longer piece of cord (220cm/86½in) so you can make two knots either side of the diamante beads.*

# Stacked Necklace

## Materials:

1m (39½in) of 0.3 gauge tiger tail wire

2 x 2mm (¹/₁₆in) silver-plated crimp beads

2 x 4mm (⅛in) silver-plated jump rings

1 x 6mm (¼in) silver-plated split ring

1 x 10mm (⅜in) silver-plated lobster clasp

112 x size 8 turquoise seed beads

24 x 13mm (½in) yellow buttons

24 x 13mm (½in) green buttons

24 x 16mm (⅝in) orange buttons

24 x 18mm (¹¹/₁₆in) purple buttons

12 x 20mm (¾in) pink buttons

## Tools:

Flat-nosed pliers

Wire cutters

Beading mat

Ruler

## Instructions:

**1** Fold the flexible beading wire in half. Place a crimp bead and jump ring over the two open ends of flexible beading wire and fold it back down the crimp bead to form a loop in which the jump ring sits. Flatten the crimp bead to secure (see diagram 3, page 7).

**2** Cut the other end of flexible beading wire open so both strands are the same length.

**3** Thread on to both strands eight seed beads and one of each coloured button in the following sequence: yellow, green, orange, purple, pink, purple, orange, green, yellow.

**4** Thread on another eight seed beads and continue this sequence of buttons and beads until they are all used or you come to the end of the flexible beading wire.

**5** Secure the end of the flexible beading wire in the same way as in step 1 with a crimp bead and jump ring.

**6** On one end of the necklace add a lobster clasp to the jump ring already attached, and on the opposite end, add a split ring.

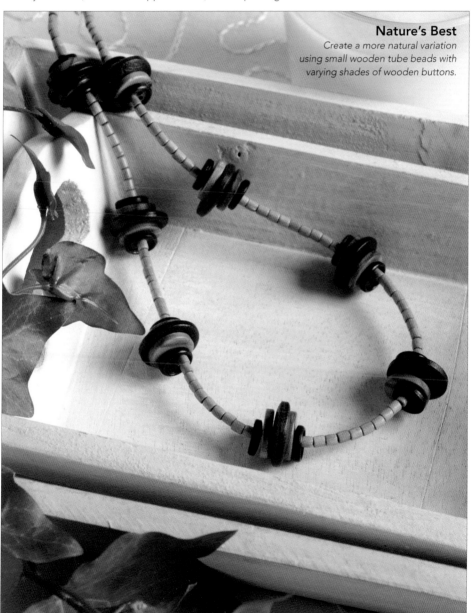

### Nature's Best
*Create a more natural variation using small wooden tube beads with varying shades of wooden buttons.*

## Publisher's Note

If you would like more information about jewellery making, try the following books in the Twenty to Make series by Search Press:
*Bracelets* by Amanda Walker, 2007,
*Charms* by Stephanie Burnham, 2007,
*Beaded Felt Jewellery* by Helen Birmingham, 2008,
*Necklaces* by Stephanie Burnham, 2008,
*Tiaras & Hairpins* by Michelle Bungay, 2008,
*Micro Macramé Jewellery* by Suzen Millodot, 2009
and *Celtic Jewellery* by Amanda Walker, 2010.

## Acknowledgement

Thanks to Francesca, Alison, Patricia and my mum for helping me to find a beautiful array of buttons. Thanks also to my friends and family for all their encouragement through all of my endeavours, and to everyone at Search Press who made this book possible. Thank you all.